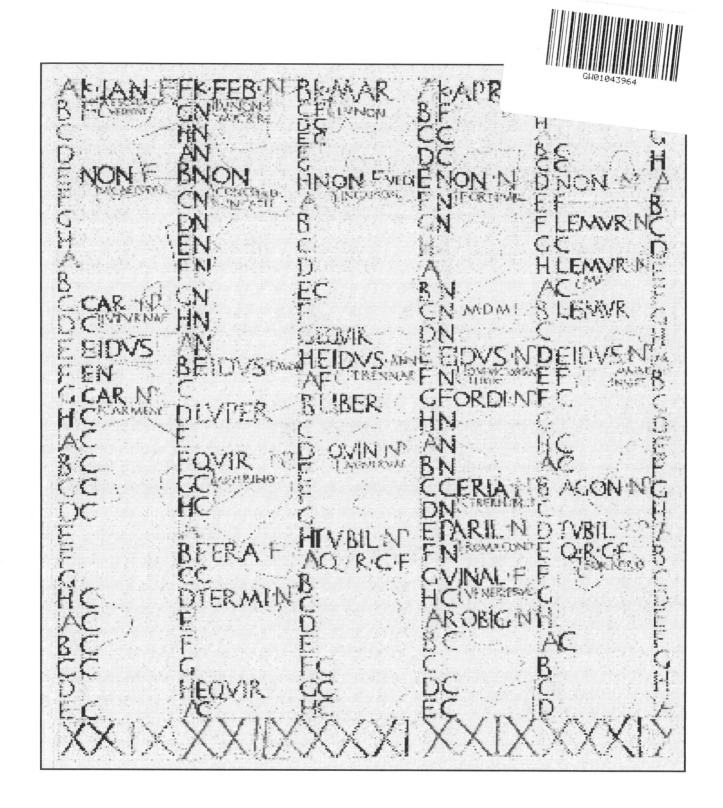

CALENDARIUM•PERPETUUM

A Modern Edition of the Ancient Roman Calendar

L•VITELLIUS•TRIARIUS

GW01043964

Copyright © 2013
Lucius Vitellius Triarius

All rights reserved.

ISBN-13: 978-1494203696
ISBN-10: 1494203693

Available from Amazon.com, CreateSpace.com, and other retail outlets

www.CreateSpace.com/4531042

Printed by CreateSpace, Charleston SC
An Amazon.com Company

TABLE OF CONTENTS

CALENDARIVM·PERPETVVM

NOTA PERSONA

Numerus	Dies	Nundinal Letter	Moribus diérum	Notae
IANVARIVS (JANUARY)				
JAN 1	Kal. Ian.	A	F	From 153 BC onward, consuls entered office on this date, accompanied by vota publica (public vows for the wellbeing of the republic and later of the emperor) and the taking of auspices. Festivals were also held for the imported cult of Aesculapius and for the obscure god Vediovis.
JAN 2	a.d. IV Non. Ian.	B	F	Ater
JAN 3	a.d. III Non. Ian.	C	C	Compitalia, a moveable feast (feriae conceptivae). In ancient Roman religion, the Compitalia (Latin: Ludi Compitalicii) was a festival celebrated once a year in honor of the Lares Compitales, household deities of the crossroads, to whom sacrifices were offered at the places where two or more ways meet. The word comes from the Latin compitum, a cross-way.
JAN 4	pr. Non. Ian.	D	C	Compitalia
JAN 5	Non. Ian.	E	F	Nones; Compitalia; Founding day of the shrine of Vica Pota on the Velian Hill
JAN 6	a.d. VIII Id. Ian.	F	F	Ater
JAN 7	a.d. VII Id. Ian.	G	C	
JAN 8	a.d. VI Id. Ian.	H	C	

CALENDARIVM•PERPETVVM

NOTA PERSONA

Numerus	Dies	Nundinal Letter	Moribus diérum	Notae
JAN 9	a.d. V Id. Ian.	A	NP	Agonalia in honor of Janus, after whom the month January is named; first of at least four festivals named Agonalia throughout the year
JAN 10	a.d. IV Id. Ian.	B	EN	
JAN 11	a.d. III Id. Ian.	C	NP	Carmentalia was the two feast days (11 Jan and 15 Jan) of the goddess Carmenta. She had her temple atop the Capitoline Hill. Carmenta was invoked in it as Postvorta and Antevorta, epithets which had reference to her power of looking back into the past and forward into the future. The festival was chiefly observed by women, with Juturna also celebrated on this day.
JAN 12	pr. Id. Ian.	D	C	
JAN 13	Id. Ian.	E	NP	Ides
JAN 14	a.d. XIX Kal. Feb.	F	EN	Ater
JAN 15	a.d. XVIII Kal. Feb.	G	NP	Carmentalia, with Juturna celebrated also on the 11th
JAN 16	a.d. XVII Kal. Feb.	H	C	
JAN 17	a.d. XVI Kal. Feb.	A	C	
JAN 18	a.d. XV Kal. Feb.	B	C	
JAN 19	a.d. XIV Kal. Feb.	C	C	
JAN 20	a.d. XIII Kal. Feb.	D	C	
JAN 21	a.d. XII Kal. Feb.	E	C	
JAN 22	a.d. XI Kal. Feb.	F	C	

CALENDARIVM·PERPETVVM

NOTA PERSONA

Numerus	Dies	Nundinal Letter	Moribus diérum	Notae
JAN 23	a.d. X Kal. Feb.	G	C	
JAN 24	a.d. IX Kal. Feb.	H	C	Sementivae, a feriae conceptivae of sowing, perhaps also known as the Paganalia as celebrated by the pagi
JAN 25	a.d. VIII Kal. Feb.	A	C	Sementivae
JAN 26	a.d. VII Kal. Feb.	B	C	Sementivae
JAN 27	a.d. VI Kal. Feb.	C	C	Dies natalis of the Temple of Castor and Pollux, or perhaps marking its rededication (see also July 15); Ludi Castores ("Games of the Castors") celebrated at Ostia during the Imperial period
JAN 28	a.d. V Kal. Feb.	D	C	
JAN 29	a.d. IV Kal. Feb.	E	C	
JAN 30	a.d. III Kal. Feb.	F	C	
JAN 31	pr. Kal. Feb.	G	C	

FEBRVARIVS (FEBRUARY)

Numerus	Dies	Nundinal Letter	Moribus diérum	Notae
FEB 1	Kal. Feb.	H	N	Kalends; Dies natalis for the Temple of Juno Sospita, Mother and Queen; sacra at the Grove of Alernus, near the Tiber at the foot of the Palatine Hill
FEB 2	a.d. IV Non. Feb.	A	N	Ater
FEB 3	a.d. III Non. Feb.	B	N	
FEB 4	pr. Non. Feb.	C	N	
FEB 5	Non. Feb.	D	N	Nones; Dies natalis for the Temple of Concordia on the Capitoline Hill
FEB 6	a.d. VIII Id. Feb.	E	N	Ater
FEB 7	a.d. VII Id. Feb.	F	N	

CALENDARIVM•PERPETVVM

NOTA PERSONA

Numerus	Dies	Nundinal Letter	Moribus diérum	Notae
FEB 8	a.d. VI Id Feb.	G	N	
FEB 9	a.d. V Id. Feb.	H	N	
FEB 10	a.d. IV Id. Feb.	A	N	
FEB 11	a.d. III Id. Feb.	B	N	
FEB 12	pr. Id. Feb.	C	N	
FEB 13	Id. Feb.	D	NP	Ides; Religiosus; Minor festival of Faunus on the Tiber Island; Parentalia, a commemoration of ancestors and the dead among families; 13th: Parentatio, with appeasement of the Manes beginning at the 6th hour and ceremonies performed by the chief Vestal; temples were closed, no fires burned on altars, marriages were forbidden, magistrates took off their insignia, until the 21st
FEB 14	a.d. XVI Kal. Mar.	E	N	Ater; Parentalia
FEB 15	a.d. XV Kal. Mar.	F	NP	Religiosus; Parentalia; Lupercalia was a very ancient, possibly pre-Roman pastoral festival, observed to avert evil spirits and purify the city, releasing health and fertility. Lupercalia subsumed Februa, an earlier-origin spring cleansing ritual held on the same date, which gives the month of February (Februarius) its name.
FEB 16	a.d. XIV Kal. Mar.	G	EN	Religiosus; Parentalia
FEB 17	a.d. XIII Kal. Mar.	H	NP	Religiosus; Parentalia; last day of the feriae conceptivae Fornacalia, the Oven

CALENDARIVM·PERPETVVM

NOTA PERSONA

Numerus	Dies	Nundinal Letter	Moribus diérum	Notae
FEB 17 (cont.)	a.d. XIII Kal. Mar.	H	NP	Festival. The Fornacalia is an Ancient Roman festival in honor of the goddess Fornax in order that the grain might be properly baked; Quirinalia, in honor of Quirinus, in which some scholars connect with the anniversary date of the murder of Romulus.
FEB 18	a.d. XII Kal. Mar.	A	C	Religiosus; Parentalia
FEB 19	a.d. XI Kal. Mar.	B	C	Religiosus; Parentalia
FEB 20	a.d. X Kal. Mar.	C	C	Religiosus; Parentalia
FEB 21	a.d. IX Kal. Mar.	D	F	Religiosus; Parentalia; Feralia, the only public observation of the Parentalia, with dark rites aimed at the gods below (di Inferi)
FEB 22	a.d. VIII Kal. Mar.	E	C	Caristia (or Cara Cognatio, "Dear Kindred"), a family pot luck in a spirit of love and forgiveness. Families gathered to dine together and offer food and incense to the Lares as their household gods. It was a day of reconciliation when disagreements were to be set aside, but the poet Ovid observes satirically that this could be achieved only by excluding family members who caused trouble.
FEB 23	a.d. VII Kal. Mar.	F	NP	Terminalia, in honor of Terminus, who was the god who protected boundary markers; his name was the Latin word for such a marker. Sacrifices were performed to sanctify each boundary

CALENDARIVM•PERPETVVM

NOTA PERSONA

Numerus	Dies	Nundinal Letter	Moribus diérum	Notae
FEB 23 (cont.)	a.d. VII Kal. Mar.	F	NP	stone, and landowners celebrated the festival in Terminus' honor each year. The Temple of Iuppiter Optimus Maximus on the Capitoline Hill was thought to have been built over a shrine to Terminus, and he was occasionally identified as an aspect of IOM under the name " Iuppiter Terminalis."
FEB 24	a.d. VI Kal. Mar.	G	N	Regifugium or Fugalia ("King's Flight") was an annual observance that took place this day each year. The Romans themselves offer varying views on the meaning of the day. According to Varro and Ovid, the festival commemorated the flight of the last king of Rome, Tarquinius Superbus, in 510 BC. Plutarch, however, explains it as the symbolic departure of the priest with the title rex sacrorum.
FEB 25	a.d. V Kal. Mar. / a.d. bis VI Kal. Mar. (Leap year)	H / G	C / N	
FEB 26	a.d. IV Kal. Mar. / a.d. V Kal. Mar.	A / H	EN / C	
FEB 27	a.d. III Kal. Mar. / a.d. IV Kal. Mar.	B / A	NP / EN	Equirria (also as Ecurria, from *equicurria, "horse races") were two ancient Roman festivals of chariot racing, or perhaps horseback racing, honoring Mars, on Feb 27 and Mar 14.

NOTA PERSONA

Numerus	Dies	Nundinal Letter	Moribus diérum	Notae
FEB 28	pr. Kal. Mar. / a.d. III Kal. Mar.	C / B	C / NP	
FEB 29	(-) / pr. Kal. Mar.	(-) / C	(-) / C	

MARTIVS (MARCH)

Numerus	Dies	Nundinal Letter	Moribus diérum	Notae
MAR 1	Kal. Mar.	D	NP	Kalends; The original Roman New Year's Day when the sacred fire of Rome was renewed; the dancing armed priesthood of the Salii celebrated the Feriae Marti (holiday for Mars), which was also the dies natalis ("birthday") of Mars; also the Matronalia, in honor of Juno Lucina, Mars' mother; Ludi Novi Romani
MAR 2	a.d. VI Non. Mar.	E	F	Ater; Ludi Novi Romani
MAR 3	a.d. V Non. Mar.	F	C	Religiosus; Ludi Novi Romani
MAR 4	a.d. IV Non. Mar.	G	C	Religiosus; Ludi Novi Romani
MAR 5	a.d. III Non. Mar.	H	C	Religiosus; Ludi Novi Romani
MAR 6	pr. Non. Mar.	A	C	Religiosus; Ludi Novi Romani
MAR 7	Non. Mar.	B	F	Nones; Religiosus; a second festival for Vediovis; Ludi Novi Romani
MAR 8	a.d. VIII Id. Mar.	C	F	Ater; Ludi Novi Romani
MAR 9	a.d. VII Id. Mar.	D	C	Religiosus; when the Salii carried the sacred shields (ancilia) around the city again; Ludi Novi Romani
MAR 10	a.d. VI Id. Mar.	E	C	Religiosus; Ludi Novi Romani
MAR 11	a.d. V Id. Mar.	F	C	Religiosus; Ludi Novi Romani
MAR 12	a.d. IV Id. Mar.	G	C	Religiosus; Ludi Novi Romani
MAR 13	a.d. III Id. Mar.	H	EN	Religiosus; Ludi Novi Romani

CALENDARIVM·PERPETVVM

NOTA PERSONA

Numerus	Dies	Nundinal Letter	Moribus diérum	Notae
MAR 14	pr. Id. Mar.	A	NP	Religiosus; the second Equirria, a Feriae Marti also called the Mamuralia or sacrum Mamurio; Ludi Novi Romani
MAR 15	Id. Mar.	B	NP	Ides; Religiosus; Feriae Iovi, sacred to Jove, and also the feast goddess Anna Perenna; Ludi Novi Romani
MAR 16	a.d. XVII Kal. Apr.	C	F	Ater
MAR 17	a.d. XVI Kal. Apr.	D	NP	Religiosus; the procession of the Argei; Liberalia, in honor of Liber; also an
				(cont.) Agonalia, or "War Festival" to Mars
MAR 18	a.d. XV Kal. Apr.	E	C	Religiosus
MAR 19	a.d. XIV Kal. Apr.	F	NP	Religiosus; Quinquatrus, later expanded into a five-day holiday as Quinquatria, a Feriae Marti, but also a feast day for Minerva, possibly because her temple on the Aventine Hill was dedicated on this day
MAR 20	a.d. XIII Kal. Apr.	G	C	Religiosus; Quinquatria
MAR 21	a.d. XII Kal. Apr.	H	C	Religiosus; Quinquatria
MAR 22	a.d. XI Kal. Apr.	A	N	Religiosus; Quinquatria
MAR 23	a.d. X Kal. Apr.	B	NP	Religiosus; Quinquatria; last day was Tubilustrium, purification of the trumpets
MAR 24	a.d. IX Kal. Apr.	C	QRCF	a day marked QRFC, when the Comitia Calata met to sanction wills
MAR 25	a.d. VIII Kal. Apr.	D	C	
MAR 26	a.d. VII Kal. Apr.	E	C	
MAR 27	a.d. VI Kal. Apr.	F	C	

CALENDARIVM·PERPETVVM

NOTA PERSONA

Numerus	Dies	Nundinal Letter	Moribus diérum	Notae
MAR 28	a.d. V Kal. Apr.	G	C	
MAR 29	a.d. IV Kal. Apr.	H	C	
MAR 30	a.d. III Kal. Apr.	A	C	
MAR 31	pr. Kal. Apr.	B	C	Anniversary of the Temple of Luna (Ave)

APRILIS (APRIL)

Numerus	Dies	Nundinal Letter	Moribus diérum	Notae
APR 1	Kal. Apr.	C	F	Kalends; Veneralia in honor of Venus. At the Veneralia, women and men asked Venus Verticordia for her help in affairs of the heart, sex, betrothal and marriage.
APR 2	a.d. IV Non. Apr.	D	F	Ater
APR 3	a.d. III Non. Apr.	E	C	
APR 4	pr. Non. Apr.	F	C	Ludi Megalenses or Megalesia, in honor of the Magna Mater or Cybele, whose temple was dedicated April 10, 191 BC
APR 5	Non. Apr.	G	N	Nones; Ludi Megalenses; anniversary of the Temple of Fortuna Publica
APR 6	a.d. VIII Id. Apr.	H	N	Ater; Ludi Megalenses
APR 7	a.d. VII Id. Apr.	A	N	Ludi Megalenses
APR 8	a.d. VI Id. Apr.	B	N	Ludi Megalenses
APR 9	a.d. V Id. Apr.	C	N	Ludi Megalenses
APR 10	a.d. IV Id. Apr.	D	N	Ludi Megalenses
APR 11	a.d. III Id. Apr.	E	N	
APR 12	pr. Id. Apr.	F	N	Cerialia or Ludi Cerialis, festival and games for Ceres, established by 202 BC
APR 13	Id. Apr.	G	NP	Ides; Ludi Cerialis; anniversary of the Temple of Jupiter Victor
APR 14	a.d. XVIII Kal. Mai.	H	N	Ater; Ludi Cerialis

CALENDARIVM·PERPETVVM

NOTA PERSONA

Numerus	Dies	Nundinal Letter	Moribus diérum	Notae
APR 15	a.d. XVII Kal. Mai.	A	NP	Ludi Cerialis; Fordicidia, offering of a pregnant cow to Tellus ("Earth")
APR 16	a.d. XVI Kal. Mai.	B	N	Ludi Cerialis
APR 17	a.d. XV Kal. Mai.	C	N	Ludi Cerialis
APR 18	a.d. XIV Kal. Mai.	D	N	Ludi Cerialis
APR 19	a.d. XIII Kal. Mai.	E	NP	Ludi Cerialis
APR 20	a.d. XII Kal. Mai .	F	N	
APR 21	a.d. XI Kal. Mai.	G	NP	Parilia, rustic festival in honor of Pales, and the dies natalis of Rome
APR 22	a.d. X Kal. Mai.	H	N	
APR 23	a.d. IX Kal. Mai.	A	F	Vinalia, he first of two wine festivals, the Vinalia Priora for the previous year's wine, held originally for Jupiter and later Venus
APR 24	a.d. VIII Kal. Mai.	B	C	
APR 25	a.d. VII Kal. Mai.	C	NP	Robigalia, an agricultural festival involving dog sacrifice
APR 26	a.d. VI Kal. Mai.	D	C	Ludi Florales in honor of Flora, extended to May 3 under the Empire
APR 27	a.d. V Kal. Mai.	E	C	Ludi Florales
APR 28	a.d. IV Kal. Mai.	F	C	Ludi Florales
APR 29	a.d. III Kal. Mai.	G	C	Ludi Florales
APR 30	pr. Kal. Mai.	H	C	Ludi Florales

MAIVS (MAY)

Numerus	Dies	Nundinal Letter	Moribus diérum	Notae
MAY 1	Kal. Mai.	A	F	Kalends; Ludi Florales; sacrifice to Maia; anniversary of the Temple of Bona Dea on the Aventine; rites for the Lares Praestites, tutelaries of the city of Rome

CALENDARIVM·PERPETVVM

NOTA PERSONA

Numerus	Dies	Nundinal Letter	Moribus diérum	Notae
MAY 2	a.d. VI Non. Mai.	B	F	Ater; Ludi Florales (under the Empire)
MAY 3	a.d. V Non. Mai.	C	C	Ludi Florales (under the Empire)
MAY 4	a.d. IV Non. Mai.	D	C	
MAY 5	a.d. III Non. Mai.	E	C	
MAY 6	pr. Non. Mai.	F	C	
MAY 7	Non. Mai.	G	F	Religiosus
MAY 8	a.d. VIII Id. Mai.	H	F	Ater
MAY 9	a.d. VII Id. Mai.	A	N	Religiosus
MAY 10	a.d. VI Id. Mai.	B	C	
MAY 11	a.d. V Id. Mai.	C	N	Religiosus
MAY 12	a.d. IV Id. Mai.	D	C	
MAY 13	a.d. III Id. Mai.	E	N	Religiosus
MAY 14	pr. Id. Mai.	F	C	Anniversary of the Temple of Mars Invictus (Mars the Unconquered); a second procession of the Argei
MAY 15	Id. Mai.	G	NP	Ides; Religiosus; Mercuralia, in honor of Mercury; Feriae of Jove
MAY 16	a.d. XVII Kal. Iun.	H	F	Ater
MAY 17	a.d. XVI Kal. Iun.	A	C	
MAY 18	a.d. XV Kal. Iun.	B	C	
MAY 19	a.d. XIV Kal. Iun.	C	C	
MAY 20	a.d. XIII Kal. Iun.	D	C	
MAY 21	a.d. XII Kal. Iun.	E	NP	One of four Agonalia, probably a third festival for Vediovis
MAY 22	a.d. XI Kal. Iun.	F	N	
MAY 23	a.d. X Kal. Iun.	G	NP	A second Tubilustrium; Feriae for Vulcanus (Vulcan)
MAY 24	a.d. IX Kal. Iun.	H	QRCF	QRCF, following Tubilustrium as in March

CALENDARIVM·PERPETVVM

NOTA PERSONA

Numerus	Dies	Nundinal Letter	Moribus diérum	Notae
MAY 25	a.d. VIII Kal. Iun.	A	C	Anniversary of the Temple of Fortuna Primigenia
MAY 26	a.d. VII Kal. Iun.	B	C	
MAY 27	a.d. VI Kal. Iun.	C	C	
MAY 28	a.d. V Kal. Iun.	D	C	
MAY 29	a.d. IV Kal. Iun.	E	C	
MAY 30	a.d. III Kal. Iun.	F	C	
MAY 31	pr. Kal. Iun.	G	C	

IVNIVS (JUNE)

Numerus	Dies	Nundinal Letter	Moribus diérum	Notae
JUN 1	Kal. Iun.	H	N	Kalends; anniversaries of the Temple of Juno Moneta; of the Temple of Mars on the clivus (slope, street) outside the Porta Capena; and possibly of the Temple of the Tempestates (storm goddesses); also a festival of the complex goddess Cardea or Carna
JUN 2	a.d. IV Non. Iun.	A	F	Ater
JUN 3	a.d. III Non. Iun.	B	C	Anniversary of the Temple of Bellona
JUN 4	pr. Non. Iun.	C	C	Anniversary of the restoration of the Temple of Hercules Custos
JUN 5	Non. Iun.	D	N	Religiosus; Anniversary of the Temple of Dius Fidius
JUN 6	a.d. VIII Id. Iun.	E	N	Ater
JUN 7	a.d. VII Id. Iun.	F	N	Religiosus; Ludi Piscatorii, "Fishermen's Games" in the Tiber River; Vestalia, in honor of Vesta
JUN 8	a.d. VI Id. Iun.	G	N	Religiosus; Vestalia; anniversary of the Temple of Mens

CALENDARIVM·PERPETVVM

NOTA PERSONA

Numerus	Dies	Nundinal Letter	Moribus diérum	Notae
JUN 9	a.d. V Id. Iun.	H	N	Religiosus; Vestalia; June 9 was a dies religiosus to her
JUN 10	a.d. IV Id. Iun.	A	N	Religiosus; Vestalia
JUN 11	a.d. III Id. Iun.	B	N	Religiosus; Vestalia; Matralia in honor of Mater Matuta; also the anniversary of the Temple of Fortuna in the Forum Boarium
JUN 12	pr. Id. Iun.	C	N	Religiosus; Vestalia
JUN 13	Id. Iun.	D	NP	Ides; Religiosus; Vestalia; Feriae of Jove; Quinquatrus minusculae, the lesser Quinquatrus celebrated by tubicines
JUN 14	a.d. XVIII Kal. Quint.	E	N	Ater; Vestalia; Quinquatrus minusculae
JUN 15	a.d. XVII Kal. Quint.	F	QSDF	Vestalia; Quinquatrus minusculae
JUN 16	a.d. XVI Kal. Quint.	G	C	
JUN 17	a.d. XV Kal. Quint.	H	C	
JUN 18	a.d. XIV Kal. Quint.	A	C	
JUN 19	a.d. XIII Kal. Quint.	B	C	A commemoration involving the Temple of Minerva on the Aventine, which had its anniversary March 19
JUN 20	a.d. XII Kal. Quint.	C	C	Anniversary of the Temple of Summanus
JUN 21	a.d. XI Kal. Quint.	D	C	
JUN 22	a.d. X Kal. Quint.	E	C	
JUN 23	a.d. IX Kal. Quint.	F	C	
JUN 24	a.d. VIII Kal. Quint.	G	C	Festival of Fors Fortuna, which "seems to have been a rowdy affair"

CALENDARIVM·PERPETVVM

NOTA PERSONA

Numerus	Dies	Nundinal Letter	Moribus diérum	Notae
JUN 25	a.d. VII Kal. Quint.	H	C	
JUN 26	a.d. VI Kal. Quint.	A	C	
JUN 27	a.d. V Kal. Quint.	B	C	Poorly attested observance in honor of the Lares; anniversary of the Temple of Jupiter Stator
JUN 28	a.d. IV Kal. Quint.	C	C	
JUN 29	a.d. III Kal. Quint.	D	C	Anniversary of the Temple of Hercules Musarum, Hercules of the Muses
JUN 30	pr. Kal. Quint.	E	C	

QVINTILIS (JULY)

Numerus	Dies	Nundinal Letter	Moribus diérum	Notae
JUL 1	Kal. Quint.	F	N	Kalends; Religiosus; a scarcely attested anniversary of a temple to Juno Felicitas
JUL 2	a.d. VI Non. Quint.	G	N	Ater
JUL 3	a.d. V Non. Quint.	H	N	Religiosus
JUL 4	a.d. IV Non. Quint.	A	N	Religiosus
JUL 5	a.d. III Non. Quint.	B	NP	Religiosus; Poplifugia, in commemoration of the flight of the Romans, when the inhabitants of Ficuleae and Fidenae appeared in arms against them, shortly after the burning of the city by the Gauls (see Battle of the Allia); the traditional victory of the Romans, which followed, was commemorated on July 7 (called the Nonae Caprotinae as a feast of Juno Caprotina), and on the next day was the Vitulatio, supposed to mark the thank-offering of the pontifices for the event.

<table>
<tbody>
<tr><td colspan="5" align="center">NOTA PERSONA</td></tr>
</tbody>
</table>

Numerus	Dies	Nundinal Letter	Moribus diérum	Notae
JUL 5 (cont.)	a.d. III Non. Quint.	B	NP	Macrobius, who wrongly places the Poplifugia on the nones, says that it commemorated a flight before the Tuscans, while Dionysius refers its origin to the flight of the people when Romulus disappeared from the earth.
JUL 6	pr. Non. Quint.	C	N	Religiosus; Ludi Apollinares, games in honor of Apollo, first held in 212 BC as a one-day event (July 13) and established as annual in 208 BC; anniversary of the Temple of Fortuna Muliebris
JUL 7	Non. Quint.	D	N	Nones; Religiosus; Ludi Apollinares; Nonae Caprotinae; Ancillarum Feriae (Festival of the Serving Women); sacrifice to Consus by unspecified public priests (sacerdotes publici); also a minor festival to the two Pales
JUL 8	a.d. VIII Id. Quint.	E	N	Ater; Ludi Apollinares; Vitulatio was an annual thanksgiving celebrated in ancient Rome on July 8, the day after the Nonae Caprotinae and following the Poplifugia on July 5. The Poplifugia is a lesser-known festival that was of obscure origin even for the Romans themselves; Macrobius says that it marked a Roman retreat from the Etruscans at Fidenae during the Gallic invasion, and that the Vitulatio commemorated their comeback victory. It was a dies

CALENDARIVM·PERPETVVM

NOTA PERSONA

Numerus	Dies	Nundinal Letter	Moribus diérum	Notae
JUL 8 (cont.)	a.d. VIII Id. Quint.	E	N	religiosus, a day of religious prohibition when people were to refrain from undertaking any activity other than attending to basic necessities.
JUL 9	a.d. VII Id. Quint.	F	N	Religiosus; Ludi Apollinares
JUL 10	a.d. VI Id. Quint.	G	C	Ludi Apollinares
JUL 11	a.d. V Id. Quint.	H	C	Ludi Apollinares
JUL 12	a.d. IV Id. Quint.	A	C	Ludi Apollinares
JUL 13	a.d. III Id. Quint.	B	C	Ludi Apollinares
JUL 14	pr. Id. Quint.	C	C	Mercatus, a series of markets or fairs following the Ludi Apollinares
JUL 15	Id. Quint.	D	NP	Ides; Mercatus; Transvectio equitum, a procession of cavalry
JUL 16	a.d. XVII Kal. Sex.	E	F	Mercatus
JUL 17	a.d. XVI Kal. Sex.	F	C	Mercatus; Sacrifice to Victory; Anniversary of the Temple of Honos and Virtus
JUL 18	a.d. XV Kal. Sex.	G	C	Mercatus
JUL 19	a.d. XIV Kal. Sex.	H	NP	Mercatus
JUL 20	a.d. XIII Kal. Sex.	A	C	Ludi Victoriae Caesaris, "Games of the Victorious Caesar", held annually from 45 BC
JUL 21	a.d. XII Kal. Sex.	B	NP	Ludi Victoriae Caesaris
JUL 22	a.d. XI Kal. Sex.	C	C	Ludi Victoriae Caesaris; Anniversary of the Temple of Concordia at the foot of the Capitol
JUL 23	a.d. X Kal. Sex.	D	NP	Ludi Victoriae Caesaris; Neptunalia held in honor of Neptune
JUL 24	a.d. IX Kal. Sex.	E	N	Ludi Victoriae Caesaris

CALENDARIVM•PERPETVVM

NOTA PERSONA

Numerus	Dies	Nundinal Letter	Moribus diérum	Notae
JUL 25	a.d. VII Kal. Sex.	F	NP	Ludi Victoriae Caesaris; Furrinalia, feriae publicae in honor of Furrina
JUL 26	a.d. VII Kal. Sex.	G	C	Ludi Victoriae Caesaris
JUL 27	a.d. VI Kal. Sex.	H	C	Ludi Victoriae Caesaris
JUL 28	a.d. V Kal. Sex.	A	C	Ludi Victoriae Caesaris
JUL 29	a.d. IV Kal. Sex.	B	C	Ludi Victoriae Caesaris
JUL 30	a.d. III Kal. Sex.	C	C	Ludi Victoriae Caesaris; Anniversary of the Temple of the Fortune of This Day (Fortunae Huiusque Diei)
JUL 31	pr. Kal. Sex.	D	C	

SEXTILIS (AUGUST)

Numerus	Dies	Nundinal Letter	Moribus diérum	Notae
AUG 1	Kal. Sex.	E	F	Kalends; anniversary of the Temple of Spes (Hope) in the Forum Holitorium, with commemorations also for the "two Victories" on the Palatine
AUG 2	a.d. IV Non. Sex.	F	F	Ater
AUG 3	a.d. III Non. Sex.	G	C	Supplicia canum ("punishment of the dogs") an unusual dog sacrifice and procession at the temples of Iuventas ("Youth") and Summanus, connected to the Gallic siege
AUG 4	pr. Non. Sex.	H	C	
AUG 5	Non. Sex.	A	F	Public sacrifice (sacrificium publicum) at the Temple of Salus on the Quirinal
AUG 6	a.d. VIII Id. Sex.	B	F	Ater
AUG 7	a.d. VII Id. Sex.	C	C	
AUG 8	a.d. VI Id. Sex.	D	C	
AUG 9	a.d. V Id. Sex.	E	C	Public sacrifice to Sol Indiges

CALENDARIVM·PERPETVVM

NOTA PERSONA

Numerus	Dies	Nundinal Letter	Moribus diérum	Notae
AUG 10	a.d. IV Id. Sex.	F	C	
AUG 11	a.d. III Id. Sex.	G	C	
AUG 12	pr. Id. Sex.	H	C	Sacrifice of a heifer to Hercules Invictus, with a libation from the skyphos of Hercules
AUG 13	Id. Sex.	A	NP	Ides; Nemoralia, the festival of Diana on the Aventine, with slaves given the day off to attend; Other deities honored at their temples include Vortumnus, Fortuna Equestris, Hercules Victor (or Invictus at the Porta Trigemina), Castor and Pollux, the Camenae, and Flora
AUG 14	a.d. XIX Kal. Sep.	B	F	Ater
AUG 15	a.d. XVIII Kal. Sep.	C	C	
AUG 16	a.d. XVII Kal. Sep.	D	C	
AUG 17	a.d. XVI Kal. Sep.	E	NP	Portunalia in honor of Portunes; anniversary of the Temple of Janus
AUG 18	a.d. XV Kal. Sep.	F	C	
AUG 19	a.d. XIV Kal. Sep.	G	FP	Vinalia Rustica, originally in honor of Jupiter, but later Venus
AUG 20	a.d. XIII Kal. Sep.	H	C	
AUG 21	a.d. XII Kal. Sep.	A	NP	Consualia, festival to Consus, with a sacrifice on the Aventine
AUG 22	a.d. XI Kal. Sep.	B	EN	
AUG 23	a.d. X Kal. Sep.	C	NP	Vulcanalia or Feriae Volcano in honor of Vulcan, along with sacrifices to Maia, the Nymphs in campo ("in the field"), Ops Opifera, and a Hora.

CALENDARIVM·PERPETVVM

NOTA PERSONA

Numerus	Dies	Nundinal Letter	Moribus diérum	Notae
AUG 24	a.d. IX Kal. Sep.	D	C	Religiosus; sacrifices to Luna on the Graecostasis; and the first of three days when the mysterious ritual pit called the mundus was opened
AUG 25	a.d. VIII Kal. Sep.	E	NP	Opiconsivia or Feriae Opi in honor of Ops Consivae at the Regia
AUG 26	a.d. VII Kal. Sep.	F	C	
AUG 27	a.d. VI Kal. Sep.	G	NP	Volturnalia, when the Flamen Volturnalis made a sacrifice to Volturnus
AUG 28	a.d. V Kal. Sep.	H	C	Games at the Circus Maximus (circenses) for Sol and Luna
AUG 29	a.d. IV Kal. Sep.	A	C	
AUG 30	a.d. III Kal. Sep.	B	C	
AUG 31	pr. Kal. Sep.	C	C	

SEPTEMBER

Numerus	Dies	Nundinal Letter	Moribus diérum	Notae
SEP 1	Kal. Sep.	D	F	Kalends; ceremonies for Jupiter Tonans ("the Thunderer") on the Capitolium, and Juno Regina on the Aventine
SEP 2	a.d. IV Non. Sep.	E	F	Ater
SEP 3	a.d. III Non. Sep.	F	C	
SEP 4	pr. Non. Sep.	G	C	
SEP 5	Non. Sep.	H	F	Anniversary of one of the temples to Jupiter Stator; Ludi Romani or Ludi Magni, "the oldest and most famous" of the ludi in ancient Rome
SEP 6	a.d. VIII Id. Sep.	A	F	Ater; Ludi Romani
SEP 7	a.d. VII Id. Sep.	B	C	Ludi Romani
SEP 8	a.d. VI Id. Sep.	C	C	Ludi Romani

CALENDARIVM•PERPETVVM

NOTA PERSONA

Numerus	Dies	Nundinal Letter	Moribus diérum	Notae
SEP 9	a.d. V Id. Sep.	D	C	Ludi Romani
SEP 10	a.d. IV Id. Sep.	E	C	Ludi Romani
SEP 11	a.d. III Id. Sep.	F	C	Ludi Romani
SEP 12	pr. Id. Sep.	G	N	Ludi Romani
SEP 13	Id. Sep.	H	NP	Ides; Ludi Romani; anniversary of the Temple to Jupiter Optimus Maximus; an Epulum Iovis; and an epulum to the Capitoline Triad were all held on this day
SEP 14	a.d. XVIII Kal. Oct.	A	F	Ater; Ludi Romani; Equorum probatio ("Approval of the Horses"), a cavalry parade of the Imperial period
SEP 15	a.d. XVII Kal. Oct.	B	N	Ludi Romani
SEP 16	a.d. XVI Kal. Oct.	C	C	Ludi Romani
SEP 17	a.d. XV Kal. Oct.	D	C	Ludi Romani
SEP 18	a.d. XIV Kal. Oct.	E	C	Ludi Romani
SEP 19	a.d. XIII Kal. Oct.	F	C	Ludi Romani
SEP 20	a.d. XII Kal. Oct.	G	C	Mercatus, days set aside for markets and fairs following the Ludi Romani
SEP 21	a.d. XI Kal. Oct.	H	C	Mercatus
SEP 22	a.d. X Kal. Oct.	A	C	Mercatus
SEP 23	a.d. IX Kal. Oct.	B	C	Mercatus; anniversary of the rededication of the Temple of Apollo in the Campus Martius; Latona was also honored
SEP 24	a.d. VIII Kal. Oct.	C	C	
SEP 25	a.d. VII Kal. Oct.	D	C	
SEP 26	a.d. VI Kal. Oct.	E	C	Anniversary of the Temple of Venus Genetrix vowed by Julius Caesar

CALENDARIVM•PERPETVVM

NOTA PERSONA

Numerus	Dies	Nundinal Letter	Moribus diérum	Notae
SEP 27	a.d. V Kal. Oct.	F	C	
SEP 28	a.d. IV Kal. Oct.	G	C	
SEP 29	a.d. III Kal. Oct.	H	C	
SEP 30	pr. Kal. Oct.	A	C	

OCTOBER

Numerus	Dies	Nundinal Letter	Moribus diérum	Notae
OCT 1	Kal. Oct.	B	N	Kalends; ceremonies for Fides and the Tigillum Sororium
OCT 2	a.d. VI Non. Oct.	C	F	Ater
OCT 3	a.d. V Non. Oct.	D	C	
OCT 4	a.d. IV Non. Oct.	E	C	Ieiunium Cereris, a day of fasting in honor of Ceres, instituted in 191 BC as a quinquennial observance, made annual by Augustus
OCT 5	a.d. III Non. Oct.	F	C	Religiosus; second of the three days when the mundus was opened
OCT 6	pr. Non. Oct.	G	C	
OCT 7	Non. Oct.	H	F	Nones; rites for Jupiter Fulgur (Jupiter of daytime lightning) and Juno Curitis
OCT 8	a.d. VIII Id. Oct.	A	F	Ater
OCT 9	a.d. VII Id. Oct.	B	C	Rites at shrines for the Genius Publicus, Fausta Felicitas, and Venus Victrix on the Capitolium
OCT 10	a.d. VI Id. Oct.	C	C	Ceremonies to mark a rededication of the Temple of Juno Moneta
OCT 11	a.d. V Id. Oct.	D	NP	Meditrinalia, was an obscure festival celebrated on October 11 in honor of the new vintage, which was offered in libations to the gods for the first time

CALENDARIVM·PERPETVVM

<table>
<tr><td colspan="5" align="center">NOTA PERSONA</td></tr>
<tr><td colspan="5"> </td></tr>
</table>

Numerus	Dies	Nundinal Letter	Moribus diérum	Notae
OCT 11 (cont.)	a.d. V Id. Oct.	D	NP	each year. The festival may have been so called from medendo, because the Romans then began to drink new wine, which they mixed with old and which served them instead of physic.
OCT 12	a.d. IV Id. Oct.	E	C	Augustalia, celebrated from 14 AD in honor of the divinized Augustus, established in 19 BC with a new altar and sacrifice to Fortuna Redux
OCT 13	a.d. III Id. Oct.	F	NP	Fontinalia in honor of Fons
OCT 14	pr. Id. Oct.	G	EN	Ceremonies to mark a restoration of the Temple of the Penates Dei on the Velian Hill
OCT 15	Id. Oct.	H	NP	Ides; Religiosus; October Horse sacrifice to Mars in the Campus Martius; also Feriae of Jupiter
OCT 16	a.d. XVII Kal. Nov.	A	F	Ater
OCT 17	a.d. XVI Kal. Nov.	B	C	Religiosus
OCT 18	a.d. XV Kal. Nov.	C	C	Religiosus
OCT 19	a.d. XIV Kal. Nov.	D	NP	Religiosus; Armilustrium, a dies religiosus in honor of Mars, was a festival in honor of Mars, the god of war, celebrated on this day. On this day the weapons of the soldiers were ritually purified and stored for winter. The army would be assembled and reviewed in the Circus Maximus, garlanded with flowers. The trumpets (tubae) would be played as part of the purification rites. The

CALENDARIVM·PERPETVVM

NOTA PERSONA

Numerus	Dies	Nundinal Letter	Moribus diérum	Notae
OCT 19 (cont.)	a.d. XIV Kal. Nov.	D	NP	Romans gathered with their arms and armor on the Aventine Hill, and held a procession with torches and sacrificial animals. The dancing priests of Mars known as the Salii may also have taken part in the ceremony.
OCT 20	a.d. XIII Kal. Nov.	E	C	
OCT 21	a.d. XII Kal. Nov.	F	C	
OCT 22	a.d. XI Kal. Nov.	G	C	
OCT 23	a.d. X Kal. Nov.	H	C	
OCT 24	a.d. IX Kal. Nov.	A	C	
OCT 25	a.d. VIII Kal. Nov.	B	C	
OCT 26	a.d. VII Kal. Nov.	C	C	Ludi Victoriae Sullanae, "Victory Games of Sulla", established as an annual event in 81 BC
OCT 27	a.d. VI Kal. Nov.	D	C	Ludi Victoriae Sullanae
OCT 28	a.d. V Kal. Nov.	E	C	Ludi Victoriae Sullanae
OCT 29	a.d. IV Kal. Nov.	F	C	Ludi Victoriae Sullanae
OCT 30	a.d. III Kal. Nov.	G	C	Ludi Victoriae Sullanae
OCT 31	pr. Kal. Nov.	H	C	Ludi Victoriae Sullanae

NOVEMBER

Numerus	Dies	Nundinal Letter	Moribus diérum	Notae
NOV 1	Kal. Nov.	A	F	Kalends; Ludi Victoriae Sullanae; Ludi circenses to close the Sullan Victory Games
NOV 2	a.d. IV Non. Nov.	B	F	Ater
NOV 3	a.d. III Non. Nov.	C	C	
NOV 4	pr. Non. Nov.	D	C	Ludi Plebeii, the Plebeian Games
NOV 5	Non. Nov.	E	F	Ludi Plebeii

CALENDARIVM·PERPETVVM

NOTA PERSONA

Numerus	Dies	Nundinal Letter	Moribus diérum	Notae
NOV 6	a.d. VIII Id. Nov.	F	F	Ater; Ludi Plebeii
NOV 7	a.d. VII Id. Nov.	G	C	Ludi Plebeii
NOV 8	a.d. VI Id. Nov.	H	C	Religiosus; Ludi Plebeii; third of the three days when mundus ritual pit was opened
NOV 9	a.d. V Id. Nov.	A	C	Ludi Plebeii
NOV 10	a.d. IV Id. Nov.	B	C	Ludi Plebeii
NOV 11	a.d. III Id. Nov.	C	C	Ludi Plebeii
NOV 12	pr. Id. Nov.	D	C	Ludi Plebeii
NOV 13	Id. Nov.	E	NP	Ides; Ludi Plebeii; Epulum Jovis; also ceremonies for Feronia and Fortuna Primigeniae
NOV 14	a.d. XVIII Kal. Dec.	F	F	Ater; Ludi Plebeii; a second Equorum probatio (cavalry parade), as on July 15
NOV 15	a.d. XVII Kal. Dec.	G	C	Ludi Plebeii
NOV 16	a.d. XVI Kal. Dec.	H	C	Ludi Plebeii
NOV 17	a.d. XV Kal. Dec.	A	C	Ludi Plebeii
NOV 18	a.d. XIV Kal. Dec.	B	C	Mercatus, days set aside for markets and fairs immediately following the Ludi
NOV 19	a.d. XIII Kal. Dec.	C	C	Mercatus
NOV 20	a.d. XII Kal. Dec.	D	C	Mercatus
NOV 21	a.d. XI Kal. Dec.	E	C	
NOV 22	a.d. X Kal. Dec.	F	C	
NOV 23	a.d. IX Kal. Dec.	G	C	
NOV 24	a.d. VIII Kal. Dec.	H	C	
NOV 25	a.d. VII Kal. Dec.	A	C	
NOV 26	a.d. VI Kal. Dec.	B	C	
NOV 27	a.d. V Kal. Dec.	C	C	
NOV 28	a.d. IV Kal. Dec.	D	C	

CALENDARIVM·PERPETVVM

NOTA PERSONA

Numerus	Dies	Nundinal Letter	Moribus diérum	Notae
NOV 29	a.d. III Kal. Dec.	E	C	
NOV 30	pr. Kal. Dec.	F	C	

DECEMBER

Numerus	Dies	Nundinal Letter	Moribus diérum	Notae
DEC 1	Kal. Dec.	G	N	Kalends; ceremonies at temples for Neptune and for Pietas
DEC 2	a.d. IV Non. Dec.	H	N	Ater
DEC 3	a.d. III Non. Dec.	A	N	Bona Dea rites for women only
DEC 4	pr. Non. Dec.	B	C	
DEC 5	Non. Dec.	C	F	Nones; a country festival for Faunus held by the pagi
DEC 6	a.d. VIII Id. Dec.	D	F	Ater
DEC 7	a.d. VII Id. Dec.	E	C	
DEC 8	a.d. VI Id. Dec.	F	C	Festival for Tiberinus Pater and Gaia
DEC 9	a.d. V Id. Dec.	G	C	
DEC 10	a.d. IV Id. Dec.	H	C	
DEC 11	a.d. III Id. Dec.	A	NP	Agonalia for Indiges; also the (probably unrelated) Septimontium
DEC 12	pr. Id. Dec.	B	EN	Ceremonies at the Temple of Consus on the Aventine
DEC 13	Id. Dec.	C	NP	Ides; dies natalis of the Temple of Tellus, and associated lectisternium for Ceres
DEC 14	a.d. XIX Kal. Ian.	D	F	Ater
DEC 15	a.d. XVIII Kal. Ian.	E	NP	Consualia or Feriae for Consus, the second of the year
DEC 16	a.d. XVII Kal. Ian.	F	C	
DEC 17	a.d. XVI Kal. Ian.	G	NP	Saturnalia in honor of Saturn, with the public ritual on the 17th
DEC 18	a.d. XV Kal. Ian.	H	C	Saturnalia

CALENDARIVM•PERPETVVM

NOTA PERSONA

Numerus	Dies	Nundinal Letter	Moribus diérum	Notae
DEC 19	a.d. XIV Kal. Ian.	A	NP	Saturnalia; Opalia in honor of Ops
DEC 20	a.d. XIII Kal. Ian.	B	C	Saturnalia
DEC 21	a.d. XII Kal. Ian.	C	NP	Saturnalia; Divalia in honor of Angerona; Hercules and Ceres, goddess of grain, also received a sacrifice
DEC 22	a.d. XI Kal. Ian.	D	C	Saturnalia; anniversary of the Temple of the Lares Permarini in the Porticus Minucia
DEC 23	a.d. X Kal. Ian.	E	NP	Saturnalia; Larentalia; commemorations for the temples of Diana and Juno Regina in the Circus Flaminius, and for the Tempestates; Sigillaria, the last day of the Saturnalia, devoted to gift-giving
DEC 24	a.d. IX Kal. Ian.	F	C	
DEC 25	a.d. VIII Kal. Ian.	G	C	Dies Natalis Solis Invicti ("Birthday of the Unconquered Sun"); Brumalia (both Imperial)
DEC 26	a.d. VII Kal. Ian.	H	C	
DEC 27	a.d. VI Kal. Ian.	A	C	
DEC 28	a.d. V Kal. Ian.	B	C	
DEC 29	a.d. IV Kal. Ian.	C	C	
DEC 30	a.d. III Kal. Ian.	D	C	
DEC 31	pr. Kal. Ian.	E	C	

CALENDARIVM·PERPETVVM

MODERN YEARS = AB URBE CONDITA (A.U.C.) YEARS

1998 = 2751	1999 = 2752	2000 = 2753	2001 = 2754	2002 = 2755
2003 = 2756	2004 = 2757	2005 = 2758	2006 = 2759	2007 = 2760
2008 = 2761	2009 = 2762	2010 = 2763	2011 = 2764	2012 = 2765
2013 = 2766	2014 = 2767	2015 = 2768	2016 = 2769	2017 = 2770
2018 = 2771	2019 = 2772	2020 = 2773	2021 = 2774	2022 = 2775
2023 = 2776	2024 = 2777	2025 = 2778	2026 = 2779	2027 = 2780
2028 = 2781	2029 = 2782	2030 = 2783	2031 = 2784	2032 = 2785
2033 = 2786	2034 = 2787	2035 = 2788	2036 = 2789	2037 = 2790
2038 = 2791	2039 = 2792	2040 = 2793	2041 = 2794	2042 = 2795
2043 = 2796	2044 = 2797	2045 = 2798	2046 = 2799	2047 = 2800
2048 = 2801	2049 = 2802	2050 = 2803	2051 = 2804	2052 = 2805
2053 = 2806	2054 = 2807	2055 = 2808	2056 = 2809	2057 = 2810
2058 = 2811	2059 = 2812	2060 = 2813	2061 = 2814	2062 = 2815
2063 = 2816	2064 = 2817	2065 = 2818	2066 = 2819	2067 = 2820
2068 = 2821	2069 = 2822	2070 = 2823	2071 = 2824	2072 = 2825

YEAR-TO-YEAR CONVERSIONS
MODERN YEAR TO AUC YEAR: MODERN YEAR + 753 = AUC YEAR
AUC YEAR TO MODERN YEAR: AUC YEAR – 753 = MODERN YEAR

MODERN YEARS = NUNDINAL YEARS

1998 = D	1999 = G	2000 = B	2001 = E	2002 = H
2003 = C	2004 = F	2005 = A	2006 = D	2007 = G
2008 = B	2009 = E	2010 = H	2011 = C	2012 = F
2013 = A	2014 = D	2015 = G	2016 = B	2017 = E
2018 = H	2019 = C	2020 = F	2021 = A	2022 = D
2023 = G	2024 = B	2025 = E	2026 = H	2027 = C
2028 = F	2029 = A	2030 = D	2031 = G	2032 = B
2033 = E	2034 = H	2035 = C	2036 = F	2037 = A
2038 = D	2039 = G	2040 = B	2041 = E	2042 = H
2043 = C	2044 = F	2045 = A	2046 = D	2047 = G
2048 = B	2049 = E	2050 = H	2051 = C	2052 = F
2053 =A	2054 =D	2055 = G	2056 =B	2057 = E
2058 = H	2059 = C	2060 = F	2061 = A	2062 = D
2063 = G	2064 = B	2065 = E	2066 = H	2067 =C
2068 = F	2069 = A	2070 =D	2071 = G	2072 = B

The first Market Day after the New Year (in regular sequence from
the prior year) determines the Nundinal Letter for the New Year.

The calendar used by the Ancient Romans

Years are counted *ab urbe condita (AUC)*, that is "from the founding of the city." Originally, the Roman calendar was what is now considered a lunisolar calendar. It was intended to align with both the lunar calendar and the solar calendar, through the means of intercalation.

The Kalends, the Nones, and the Ides
The Roman calendar operated through the use of three main days (the Kalends, the Nones, and the Ides), in reference to which all dates were given.

The Kalends
The Kalends (*Kalendae*), which was always the first day of the month, was sacred to Iuno. The first of the month, following the lunar part of the calendar's operation, was the day following the appearance of the New Moon. On this day, the Rex Sacrorum, together with a pontifex minor, offered a sacrifice to Iuno, and announced the date of the coming Nones, which fell on the day after the First Quarter.

The Nones
The Nones (*Nonae*), falling on either the fifth or seventh day of the month, came the day after the First Quarter of the lunar cycle. On this day, the Regina Sacrorem offered to Iuno at the Regia either a lamb or a pig, after which the feriae for the entire month were announced. Before the Nones of any given month (with the exception of the Poplifugium), no feriae publicae were held.

The Ides
Lastly, the Ides (*Idus*) came, either on the thirteenth or fifteenth day of the month, on the day after the full moon. On this day, a sacrifice was given to Iuppiter, for which reason it is commonly noted as *Feriae Iovi* in the ancient Fasti. From here, the Pontifices determined the number of days remaining until the next New Moon, which would restart the cycle. The Ides, also, were always *dies Nefasti Publici*, given their permanent status as Feriae Iovi, without exception.

Moribus diérum
or Character of Days in the Calendar

These are the rules which are pronounced by the pontifices, and breaking them is *nefas* (though it may sometimes be expiated).

Dies fasti [F]
- ordinary citizens may do anything;
- the *comitia tributa*, *concilium plebis*, and *comitia centuriata* may not be convened;
- curule magistrates may exercise their judicial functions.

Dies comitiales [C]
- similar to *dies fasti*, except that the *comitia tributa* and *centuriata*, and the *concilium plebis* may be convened.

Dies nefasti [N]
- ordinary citizens may do anything;
- proceedings of the *comitia tributa*, *concilium plebis*, and *comitia centuriata* are prohibited;
- exercise of their judicial functions by curule magistrates is prohibited.

Dies nefasti publici [NP]
- similar to *dies nefasti* with the following modifications:

  - acts of physical violence and beginning of lawsuits are nefas;
  - quarrels should be avoided (but robust and lively debate was acceptable);
  - slaves are allowed the day off work;
  - ordinary citizens should avoid any physical labour except what is urgently necessary and cannot be postponed;

- the flamines and the rex sacrorum may not see anyone doing any physical labour, and may fine anyone they see doing physical labour.

Dies endotercisi [EN]
(also called *dies intercisi*)

- same as *dies nefasti* in the morning;
- same as *dies fasti* in the afternoon;
- same as *dies nefasti* in the evening.

Dies fasti publici or principio [FP]
There are two interpretations of this designation presented by scholars. They are:

- as *dies fasti principio*:
  - same as *dies fasti* in the morning;
  - same as *dies nefasti* in the afternoon and evening.
- as *dies fasti publici*:
  - same as *dies nefasti publici*.

Quando Rex Comitiavit fas [QRCF]

- same as *dies nefasti* until the rex sacrorum appears in the comitia;
- same as *dies fasti* after that.

Quando Stercus Delatum fas [QSDF]

- same as *dies nefasti* until the Temple of Vesta has been cleaned;
- same as *dies fasti* after that

Dies atri and dies religiosi (or vitiosi)
Dies atri and dies religiosi are less formal but widely observed.

Dies atri: unlucky days;

- one should try to avoid making journeys, starting new projects, or doing anything risky;
- certain deities, including Iuppiter and Ianus, should not be named.
- these days are ill-omened to begin any new project, and any new project would necessarily begin by performing a rite calling for the assistance of the gods. Such religious rites, beginning something new, are not to be performed.
- normal work would still be performed on dies atri, and as part of performing any work one performs rites for the patron deities, geni locii, and other appropriate deities. Naturally enough, the daily routine is also performed before the lararium.

Dies religiosi (vitiosi): similar to *dies atri*:

- no private religious rites should be performed, but public rites may, subject to the same exclusions as for *dies atri*;
- try to avoid making journeys, starting new projects, or doing anything risky.

Nundinae
and the Nundinal Letters

Nundinae were originally market-days, held every eighth day, on which Romans came into the city to trade and do business. On Roman calendars the days were given nundinal letters (A to H) to help people see when the next market-day would be. The markets were held on a different day each year.

EST. 2760

VITELLIAN·TRADERS·LTD

CALENDARIVM·PERPETVVM

REFERENCES AND FURTHER READING

1. Bennett, Chris. Roman Dates Website,
    www.tyndalehouse.com/Egypt/ptolemies/chron/roman/chron_rom_intro_fr.htm

2. Bickerman, E. J. Chronology of the Ancient World. (London: Thames & Hudson, 1969, rev. ed. 1980).

3. Blackburn, Bonnie and Leofranc Holford-Strevens, The Oxford companion to the year, Oxford University Press, 1999, page 669.

4. Brind'Amour, P. Le Calendrier romain: Recherches chronologiques (Ottawa, 1983), 256–275

5. Brind'Amour, P. Le Calendrier romain: Recherches chronologiques (Ottawa, 1983)

6. Bunson, Matthew. A Dictionary of the Roman Empire (Oxford University Press, 1995), pp. 246–247; Roland Auguet, Cruelty and Civilization: The Roman Games (Routledge, 1972, 1994) pp. 212–213.

7. Cato the Elder, De agricultura 138; Columella 2.21.2; Scullard, Festivals and Ceremonies of the Roman Republic, p. 39.

8. Cicero, De legibus 2.29

9. Cicero, Republic 2.27

10. Cruelty. The Oxford Dictionary of Phrase, Saying, and Quotation, 2nd edition. Susan Ratcliffe, ed. New York: Oxford University Press, 2002,109-110

11. Feeney, Denis C. Caesar's Calendar: Ancient Time and the Beginnings of History. Berkeley: University of California Press, 2007

CALENDARIVM·PERPETVVM

12. Fowler, Warde. The Roman festivals of the period of the republic (London, 1899/1908), p.5

13. Holleran, Claire. Shopping in Ancient Rome: The Retail Trade in the Late Republic and the Principate (Oxford University Press, 2012), pp. 189–190, 193

14. http://bmcr.brynmawr.edu/1997/97.08.07.html

15. Humphrey, John H. Roman Circuses: Arenas for Chariot Racing (University of California Press, 1986), p. 543; Robert Turcan, The Gods of Ancient Rome (Edinburgh University Press, 2000), p. 82.

16. Inscriptiones Italiae XIII.2.377

17. Livy, 43.11.13

18. Livy, 45.44.3

19. Livy. Ab urbe condita, 1:31

20. Livy. History of Rome 1.19

21. Macrobius. Saturnalia 1.16.2

22. Macrobius. Saturnalia, tr. Percival Vaughan Davies, book I, chapters 12–13, pp. 89–95

23. Michels, A. K. The Calendar of the Roman Republic (Princeton, 1967)

24. Mommsen, Theodor. History of Rome, Book I chapter 14

25. Ovid. Fasti, tr. A. S. Kline (2004), Book II

26. Plutarch. Life of Numa, chapter 18

27. Plutarch. Numa Pompilius "Plutarch: excerpt from Numa Pompilius"

28. Religio Section, Nova Roma Website, www.novaroma.org.

29. Richards, E. G. Mapping Time. Oxford: Oxford University Press.

30. Rüpke, J. The Roman Calendar from Numa to Constantine: Time, History, and the Fasti, pp. 26–27

31. Scheid, John. "To Honour the Princeps and Venerate the Gods: Public Cult, Neighbourhood Cults, and Imperial Cult in Augustan Rome," translated by Jonathan Edmondson, pp. 288–290

32. Scullard, H. H. Festivals and Ceremonies of the Roman Republic (Cornell University Press, 1981)

33. Smith, William (ed.). A Dictionary of Greek and Roman Antiquities, John Murray, London, 1875

34. Varro, Marcus Terentius. De lingua latina 6.12; 6:27

35. Wagenvoort, Hendrik. "Initia Cereris," in Studies in Roman Literature, Culture and Religion (Brill, 1956), pp. 163–164

ABOUT THE AUTHOR

The author, Lucius Vitellius Triarius, aka Chip Hatcher, is a Graduate (cum Laude) in Political Science, focusing in Ancient Mediterranean Political Systems, from the University of Tennessee at Knoxville and resides in the foothills of the Great Smoky Mountains in Eastern Tennessee.

He is also a member of Nova Roma (www.novaroma.org), the global Roman Reconstruction project, advocating the via Romana, or Roman Way, where he serves as a Provincial Governor and Senator of Nova Roma.

The Roman Way is the study and practical application of "Romanitas" and the "mos maiorum", the revival of all aspects of Roman life, culture, virtues, ethics and philosophies in our everyday lives.

It is as part of the mos maiorum that citizens are expected to take up Roman names for use within the society. Learning Latin, the language of Roman culture, is also an equally important step towards becoming a modern Roman.

One of the cornerstones of Romanitas are the Roman virtues; those qualities which define the ideal state of being and behavior of the Roman citizen. These age old precepts guided the Roman Republic for centuries, and after being somewhat forgotten in the technology, hustle, and bustle of the modern age, are finding their way back into the hearts, minds, and homes of many people today. They are the foundation of a good and wholesome society, and should be consistently used to further advance the knowledge, behavior and ethics of our children and succeeding generations.

He believes that we must remember and preserve the good parts of the past in the present, so that others will remember it in the future.

Printed in Great Britain
by Amazon

16537887R00023